WHITE LIES, BLACK BLOOD

The Awful Killing of Kipper Billy

KEN BLANCH

WARNING: This book describes incidents and contains images involving deceased Aboriginal persons. Language and terms used in quoted accounts may offend some readers. The publishers respectfully acknowledge the traditional country across the region in which we live and work. We acknowledge and pay our respects to the Kabi Kabi, Jinibara and Turrbal Traditional Custodians, and their elders past, present and emerging.

Contents

Foreword to second edition, 2024

OUR DAD, Ken Blanch OAM, was indefatigable. After a more-than-50-year journalistic career that earned him an Order of Australia Medal, he busied himself in retirement pursuing "cold case" stories he had either covered as a Brisbane reporter or happened upon for his *Sunday Mail* column, *The Way We Were.*

"Blanchy", as he was known among colleagues in newsrooms, spent countless hours in the Queensland State Archives researching these passion projects. Among them was the tragic case of Indigenous man Kipper Billy, a convicted rapist condemned to hang in 1862 before a watertight alibi was established for him and his co-accused, Billy Horton. While Horton was pardoned before the execution could be carried out, no such acknowledgment of innocence was extended to Kipper Billy, who had been killed during an attempted jailbreak.

Ken was ever ready to fight injustice, despite his hard-bitten persona. He told us his heart "always beat a little harder" for Kipper Billy. His dogged delving resulted in the self-published first edition of this book *White Lies, Black Blood: The Awful Killing of Kipper Billy* in 2015.

And that resulted in an historic posthumous pardon for Kipper Billy by the Governor of Queensland in 2018. Dad was then 90.

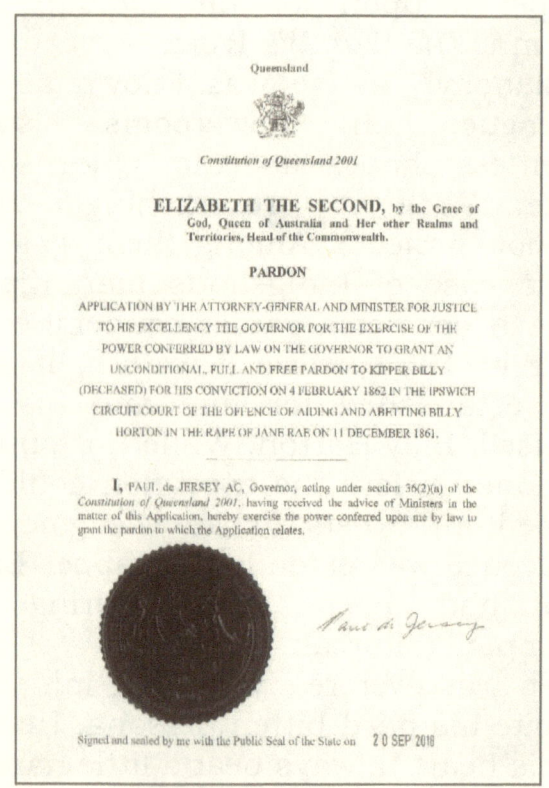

Queensland

Constitution of Queensland 2001

ELIZABETH THE SECOND, by the Grace of God, Queen of Australia and Her other Realms and Territories, Head of the Commonwealth.

PARDON

APPLICATION BY THE ATTORNEY-GENERAL AND MINISTER FOR JUSTICE TO HIS EXCELLENCY THE GOVERNOR FOR THE EXERCISE OF THE POWER CONFERRED BY LAW ON THE GOVERNOR TO GRANT AN UNCONDITIONAL, FULL AND FREE PARDON TO KIPPER BILLY (DECEASED) FOR HIS CONVICTION ON 4 FEBRUARY 1862 IN THE IPSWICH CIRCUIT COURT OF THE OFFENCE OF AIDING AND ABETTING BILLY HORTON IN THE RAPE OF JANE RAE ON 11 DECEMBER 1861.

I, PAUL de JERSEY AC, Governor, acting under section 36(2)(a) of the *Constitution of Queensland 2001*, having received the advice of Ministers in the matter of this Application, hereby exercise the power conferred upon me by law to grant the pardon to which the Application relates.

Signed and sealed by me with the Public Seal of the State on 2 0 SEP 2018

While he was gratified by his career accolades – Walkley and Clarion recognition for his outstanding contribution to journalism and his most valued, a union Gold Honour Badge – by his death at 92 Ken said he had satisfied his last journalistic endeavour: restoring the reputation of a man who had paid a terrible price for a crime he did not commit.

We, his daughters, have always been proud of our father's achievements, and are delighted that his forensic examination of true crime has been amplified in popular culture.

First, Ken's *The Taxi Driver Killer: The Southport Murder*[1], was cited and used by Brisbane writer Trent Dalton in his 2019 novel *Boy Swallows Universe*.

The character of Arthur "Slim" Halliday, dubbed "The Houdini of Boggo Road", was central to Dalton's narrative.

Dalton's best-selling memoir-thriller was published by HarperCollins, subsequently adapted for the stage by Tim McGarry and performed by the Queensland Theatre Company in 2021 and, most recently, adapted by John

---

[1] Jack Sim Publications, order online at www.jacksim.com.au

Collee as a TV series, which started its Netflix streaming run as an all-star serialised drama in January 2024.

Second, Ken's self-published version of this book, *White Lies, Black Blood*, was cited and used by Miles Franklin Award winning-author Melissa Lucashenko in her 2023 novel, *Edenglassie* (UQP), subsequently winner of the Victorian Premier's Literary Awards 2024 (fiction) and shortlisted for the Indie Book Awards 2024.

Kelyn Flynn and Marie Blanch
May 2024

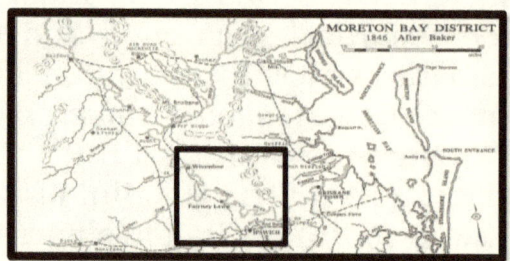

Map of Moreton Bay District in 1846 showing pastoral runs selected after 1842. Early events in this book were located near "Fairney Lawn" (also Ferny or Fernie Lawn), a run owned by the North family and situated on the Brisbane River near Ipswich. The enclosed area shows the "Fairney Lawn" in relation to Wivenhoe and Ipswich. (Moreton Bay District 1846 after Baker, with additions. Author's alterations.)

Chapter 1, Rape on the river bend

MORE than 150 years have passed since two Indigenous men (then named "Billy Horton" and "Kipper Billy" by the new colonial-settlers of Moreton Bay) were arrested and charged with the rape of a married woman on the banks of the Brisbane River at a place then called Fairney Lawn (also Ferny or Fernie Lawn), near the now trendy Ipswich dormitory village of Fernvale.

But no amount of time can dim the inhuman treatment of the two innocent Indigenous men who were sentenced to death by white law for the attack on the woman, Mrs Jane Rae.

Both Aboriginal men thwarted the hangman: one by dying in an attempted prison escape and the other by being pardoned just minutes after witnessing the appalling execution of a fellow prisoner, which he believed to be a macabre rehearsal of the fate that awaited *him*.

The survivor, Billy Horton, was pardoned unconditionally when it was found, while he was daily awaiting the attentions of the hangman, that he had an unassailable alibi for the time of the rape. But, although new evidence indicating Kipper Billy's innocence of the charge of having aided and abetted Billy Horton was already known, the reprieve came too late for him – he had died 31 days before at the walls of Brisbane Gaol in what must be one of the most bizarre deaths in custody ever recorded.

And even that is not the end of Kipper Billy's story. There is more, much more, to the story of this young, 19th century Indigenous man than merely the callous official indifference that had denied him justice for all those years.

His story has been reimagined – with full credit to this book and its author, Ken Blanch – in the 2023 release, *Edenglassie*, by Miles Franklin award-winning Goorie author Melissa Lucashenko (published by University of Queensland Press).

Lucashenko has renamed Kipper Billy "Mulanyin" and woven his life into a tale of early Brisbane which extends to the present day.

And it all began on the tranquil banks of the Wivenhoe reach of the Upper Brisbane River as Mrs Rae, who had been doing her laundry in the river outside the family's pioneer hut, boiled the kettle to make lunch for her husband, son and daughter on a noon day a couple of weeks before Christmas 1861.

※※※

ACCORDING to Mrs Rae, two Indigenous men (she and all the colonial settler reports referred to them as "blacks") emerged from the bush as she went to a sawpit 30 metres from the hut to get some wood chips for the cooking fire.

In her testimony against Kipper Billy, she told the Supreme Court at Ipswich on February 4, 1862:

> *I reside 4 miles (6½ kilometres) from Fernie Lawn. On a Wednesday a fortnight or so before Christmas something happened to me. In the forenoon of that day, I was washing in the (Brisbane) river. I went up to my hut to put the kettle on the fire for dinner. I put the kettle on the fire, and I then went down to the sawpit to get some chips.*

I saw a bag of sugar by the edge of the scrub. I took the bag of sugar up and was carrying it up to the hut. When I got very near the hut, a blackfellow came behind me and caught me by the hair of the head. He asked me what I was going to do with that bag of sugar.

The blackfellow was Johnny Stinkabed. He had been at the sawpit the Saturday before. He spoke to me. The prisoner (Kipper Billy) came up after Johnny Stinkabed spoke to me.

The prisoner asked me where my daughter was. He asked me where "young fellow Mary" was. I did not tell him where she really was. I said she was down at the river. Both blacks spoke at once and said I was a bloody liar and that she was at old Joe North's.

Mrs Rae continued:

After they had told me I was a bloody liar, the prisoner and Stinkabed Johnny pulled me down on the ground. The prisoner laid hold of my arm and the other laid hold of me across the neck. While I was down, I saw another blackfellow jump across the sawpit at the edge of the scrub. He came up to me while I was on the ground.

This third blackfellow was dressed. I think he had a pair of trousers on. The trousers were unfastened and he was holding them up with his hand. The third blackfellow took up my clothes. He had connection with me the same as my husband. He put his private parts into mine. I am quite sure of that, in the same way as my husband has connection with me.

The prisoner and Johnny Stinkabed later dragged me down to the riverbank. The prisoner held me down by my legs while Stinkabed Johnny tried to have connection with me. I screamed as loud as I was able, and I heard the sound of a horse's feet in the river. The prisoner and Johnny let me go. The last I saw of the third blackfellow who committed the capital offence was when I saw him sitting on the bag of sugar by the hut.

I saw a blackfellow afterwards in one of the cells at Ipswich. I knew him then. Billy Horton is the man. I saw my son after this occurred. I complained to my son. I did not see the prisoner afterwards until he was brought to my house on horseback by Mr Pritchard's black men. This was some time afterwards.

I am sure the prisoner was the man who held me by the arm while Billy Horton was committing the offence and also the man who held me by the legs at the river.

Under cross-examination by Mr Bramston, who defended Kipper Billy, Mrs Rae said:

I never saw the prisoner to my knowledge before that day. There was nothing particular about him. He was naked. Stinkabed Johnny had no clothes on. He had an old rag or something over his face with two holes that he could see out of. He had it tied around his neck with a piece of bark. The prisoner had nothing on his face. Stinkabed Johnny asked me if I knew him and I said no, and he asked me again and I still said no.

The blacks do not often come to my place. I do not suppose that Billy Horton was on the top of me for more than a minute or a minute and a half. It might not have been so much as a minute. Billy Horton came out of the scrub the moment I was pulled down. The sawpit is about 30 yards from the house. I dropped the bag of sugar when the blackfellow first seized me. Stinkabed Johnny told me to drop it as there was no fear of taking it away. I said nothing but put it down. They did not take it away with them.

The prisoner and Johnny Stinkabed pulled Billy Horton off me by the hair of the head. I did not tell my son that I had been ravished. I told it first to Sergeant Carson. I was in Ipswich and unable to go home and I told him. I don't remember whether I complained to anyone about what was done at the river.

I came to town on the Wednesday evening, and when I came to town

I had to be assisted into a bed. The next day I applied for a warrant. I had not told Sergeant Carson then. I did not tell the whole story because my husband was with me, and I knew what sort of a disposition he had, and I did not wish to have a disturbance with him. My husband followed me, and I had no chance of saying anything without him knowing it.

After my husband went home, I went to Mr Carson's house. My husband went home on the Thursday afternoon. I think I went to Mr Carson's house on the Sunday afternoon. When Kipper Billy was brought to me in the hut, I recognised him. He never spoke. I had a right to know him. There is a difference on all blackfellows. I am positive he is the same man.

Mrs Rae said she was not examined by a doctor. Her son, Edward Rae, 17, swore that as he was crossing the Brisbane River on December 11, 1861, he heard screams. "I stopped and heard them plainer," he said. "I pushed on, and I saw my mother tying a stockwhip about an old breeding mare's neck. Her hair was hanging down her back, her dress was very nearly torn off, and her arms were bleeding. I went to her and when I got up to her, she said something to me. I then went to the house. I afterwards came back to my mother. In about 20 minutes I went on to Mr Pritchard's and saw him."

James Pritchard was the publican at Wivenhoe. He knew the prisoner, he said, as Kipper Billy. On December 10 or 11, 1861, he saw Edward Rae and he later saw the prisoner. "He (Kipper Billy) was not there when young Rae came, but he came a little while afterwards," Pritchard said. "I saw Kipper Billy about 50 yards from my house. He was with other blacks. I spoke to them and asked them to catch some fish for me. Young Rae came to me (again) on a Wednesday about a month or more afterwards. I apprehended the prisoner with the assistance of two blackfellows. After I apprehended the prisoner, I took him to Mrs Rae's. She identified him in my presence."

Pritchard said he did not know Kipper Billy before December 1861.

"When I spoke to the prisoner, he was 50 yards (46 metres) off," he said. "I had heard his name before. I arrested him because Mr Bigge and Mr North said they wished him to be apprehended, as they believed he was the ringleader of the affair. He was the same man who came to my house on the same day young Rae called and to whom I gave fishing lines. He came about one or two o'clock in the day. I am 4 miles (7 kilometres) from Mr Rae. When I saw Kipper Billy on the same day young Rae came to my house, he had trousers and shirt on."

There were peculiar aspects to the story, which the witnesses told twice on the same day as Kipper Billy and Billy Horton underwent separate trials. Mrs Rae said one of the Aboriginal men pulled the rapist off her. Another had accused her of telling the police he was "Nelson", a well-known troublemaker, but said he was not. She said the only one of the Indigenous men she knew was "Stinkabed Johnny".

Mrs Rae said she had screamed as loudly as she could, and when her son came across the river on horseback the Aboriginal men dived in and swam to the other side. When she tried to get up the riverbank, she found she had lost the use of one foot. Mrs Rae described one of the Indigenous men and the clothes he wore, which included a clean blue Scottish twill shirt and trousers. Police Sergeant William Carson arrested Billy Horton when he saw him under a dray at Fernie Lawn after identifying him from Mrs Rae's description. Edward Rae said he did not see any Indigenous men but fetched his sister from the river. When he returned to his mother after about 20 minutes, she was raving and screaming and trying to drag the family mare to the river.

Kipper Billy was charged with aiding and abetting Billy Horton. Mrs Rae identified him as the Indigenous man who had pulled Billy Horton off her. The defence was to tell the jury that Kipper Billy's action in pulling Billy Horton off Mrs Rae seemed a strange way to assist him, but the jurors took only a few minutes to find both men guilty.

Through an interpreter, Kipper Billy told the trial judge, Alfred Lutwyche, only that he was not guilty. Billy Horton addressed the judge without assistance and told him: "Your Honour and members of the jury, this woman came before magistrates one time, she say me not blackfellow (who attacked her) at all; another time she come before magistrates and said me be blackfellow who did it."

The judge, with the traditional square of black cloth atop his judicial wig, addressed the two hapless men in sombre tones:

Billy Horton, you have been found guilty by the verdict of a jury of rape upon the person of Jane Rae, and you, Kipper Billy, of aiding and abetting Billy Horton in his crime. The sentence I shall pronounce upon you is the sentence of the law, namely that you be taken from where you are now to the place from whence you came, that you be taken thence to the common gaol in Brisbane, and that there, on such day as it shall please His Excellency the Governor, with the advice of his Executive Council, to appoint, you shall be led to the place of execution, and be there hanged by the neck until you are dead. And may God have mercy on your souls.

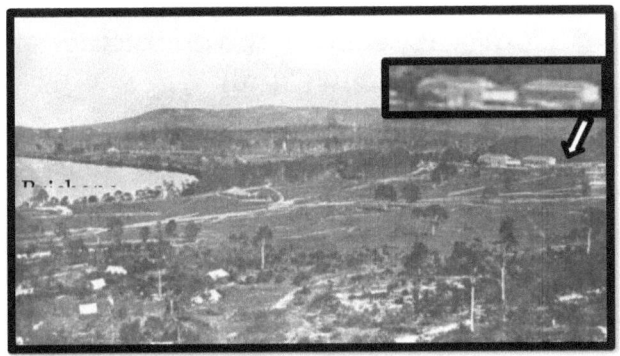

HM Gaol, Brisbane, which was located at what is now The Barracks Precinct, Petrie Terrace, photographed from the Wickham Terrace windmill in 1862. Inset: closer view of the gaol. (State Library of Qld; # 61766)

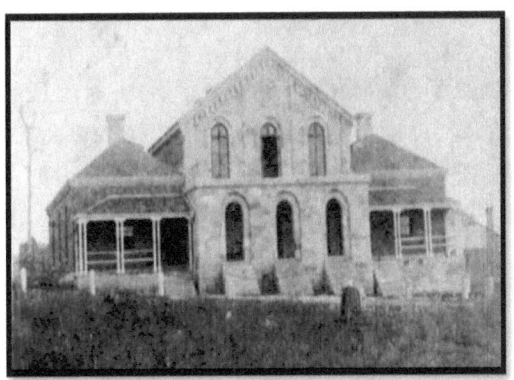

Old Ipswich Courthouse where Judge Lutwyche condemned Billy Horton and Kipper Billy. (State Library of Qld; #89244)

Chapter 2, A judge agrees

JOHNNY Stinkabed disappeared from the scene of the crime and was not seen again. A report in Brisbane's then-*Courier* newspaper (a forerunner of *The Courier-Mail*[2]) sometime afterwards suggested he had been shot by Indigenous police near their camp at Wivenhoe and buried in the bush.

Judge Lutwyche wrote in his official notes on the proceedings: "The jury found both prisoners guilty, and I concur in their verdict. The presence of Billy Horton on the scene at the moment when Mrs Rae was thrown upon the ground can hardly be ascribed to accident, and I think that there can be no reasonable doubt that there had been a previous arrangement between these blackfellows that all of them should violate her person, though they might not have agreed that Billy Horton should be the first to violate her. But even on a technical point of view the actual assistance given to Billy

---

[2] Three newspapers called *Courier* were published in Brisbane during the 19th century: *The Moreton Bay Courier* 1846-May 1861; *The Courier* May 1861-April 1864; *The Brisbane Courier* April 1864-1933.

Horton by the other two blackfellows was evidence to go to the jury of the intent to assist, and I think they (the jury) came to the right conclusion." The trials of Kipper Billy and Billy Horton were not the first dual rape trials presided over by Judge Lutwyche. In June 1859, only months before Queensland was separated from New South Wales to become an independent colony, the judge presided over the trials of two Aboriginal men named Chamery and Dick who also were accused of raping a white woman when they visited her, naked, at a lonely hut at Dugandine, near Ipswich. At those trials the defence relied heavily on the need for positive identification of the culprits, and the judge was at pains to point out to the jurors the need for them to cast aside any prejudice they had against Aboriginal people.

Chamery had supposedly stated to Lieutenant Williams, of the native police: "What a stupid head mine must be to ravish a white woman." Judge Lutwyche interpreted this as an admission of guilt but told the jury: "I have heard with some surprise of prejudice existing against blackfellows in this district. But you must each remember that he, the prisoner, is as much a subject of the Queen as you are … and you will judge the prisoner as you would a British born subject."

In each case the juries took only a short retirement to find the prisoners guilty. In reporting the trials, *The Moreton Bay Courier* observed that "His Honour was visibly affected at the dread sentence he was called upon to pass and sat for a few moments evidently the subject of strong emotions".

His Honour apparently found nothing incongruous in the alleged use of the sophisticated English verb "ravish" by Chamery, a traditional man who still went naked among whites, to describe his crime. When asked whether they had anything to say before being sentenced to death, both men denied guilt and said they knew nothing about the rape. They were subsequently hanged in the old Brisbane Gaol in Queen Street on unscreened gallows that could be seen from vantage points outside the prison, although public executions had been officially banned five years before.

The Courier was not impressed with the conviction of Billy Horton and Kipper Billy on the uncorroborated evidence of the victim, and outspokenly advocated a change in the law of evidence relating to rape. On February 17, 1862, it said in a bold editorial:

The case of Billy Horton, the Aboriginal who lies condemned to death in Her Majesty's Gaol, is a very peculiar one. It is a fearful, but perhaps necessary, protection which the law allows to a woman, to establish a capital charge against a man by her unsupported testimony. Also, there is so much in the manner in which she gives her evidence that it is not easy for persons who are not present at a trial of this kind to judge with accuracy what degree of credence a jury is justified in giving to her statements.

We should be disposed to insist on a slight modification of the law here. For assault, we would leave the law as to evidence as it stands. But in regard to the capital offence, we do think some strong corroborative evidence should be required. In this particular instance, of course, it is only a blackfellow who, at the worst, stands in danger of having his life taken away through a mistake as to his features; but, while with a certain stamp of casuists who are occasionally to be met with in this colony such a distinction may make all the difference in the world, to us the life of an innocent black man is an object of some importance. We shall therefore briefly advert to some features in this case, premising that, above all things, a jury should be perfectly satisfied, and satisfied beyond even a shadow of a doubt, of the consistency, value and truthfulness of the prosecutrix's evidence.

The Courier continued to detail the flaws in the case:

In the first place, blackfellows are not easily identified. Mrs Rae did not know Billy Horton previously. When discovered by her son about 20 minutes after her ill-treatment, she was raving, and immediately after became insensible. She had at once complained to her son of some blackfellows having "beaten" her. The same day on which the offence was committed she went into Ipswich to make a complaint. This she did with the knowledge, and therefore, with the consent, of her husband. She made the complaint; the Police Magistrate took her sworn information; and what did she swear?

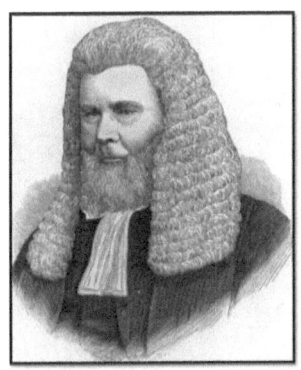

Judge Alfred Lutwyche (State Library of Qld; #21331)

In that information, assault with intent was charged, but not rape. When before the bench, and faced with Billy Horton, she distinctly stated – but not on oath – that he was present but had not assaulted her in any way. Whether the "peculiar disposition of her husband" had changed in the interval, whether she found courage to tell him of the real nature of the offence committed, and his peculiar disposition caused him to desire that she should do stern justice, does not appear, but a week or two after she made a second journey to Ipswich to lodge a very different complaint – a charge of rape – against Billy Horton, who was the only black in custody. The one black whose name she did know at the time the offence was committed has never been found. In her first information this black, who has not been found, appeared as the principal offender. So much for the consistency, the truthfulness, the value of the prosecutrix's evidence.

Billy Horton was apprehended by a constable sent in search of another blackfellow, differently named in the warrant, and charged with a very different offence, on the strength of his being near the spot *from which the blackfellows who ill-treated Mrs Rae had fled, and being dressed in similar clothes – a blue Scotch twill shirt, and blue serge or flannel trousers, of the kind usually given to blackfellows. But all this goes to prove his innocence of the crime, and only raises a suspicion of his having assisted the escape of the real offender by changing clothes with him.*

Billy Horton is possibly a rogue. He is well known, and very well known to the inhabitants of Ipswich and to the police there. He bears more than an average good character for a black man. He has never been accused of this kind of offence before. We believe that evidence is procurable to show that Billy Horton was at a considerable distance from the spot when Mrs Rae was assaulted. In the meantime, we commend the above peculiar circumstances of the case, which lie on the surface of it, to the attention of His Excellency (the Governor, Sir George Bowen) and the Executive Council.

The evidence *The Courier* quoted as "procurable" had been foreshadowed in *The Queensland Times* published in Ipswich 10 days before. That newspaper had reported that the Burnett mailman, a man named Thomas Birch, was prepared to make an affidavit swearing that he saw Billy Horton, whom he knew well, 11 miles (18 kilometres) away from the scene near the time the rape of Mrs Rae occurred. This suggestion that Billy Horton had an alibi for the time of the crime had therefore been known publicly, at the time of *The Courier* editorial, for some 10 days without any official action being taken to confirm it while the two black men endured the horror of daily awaiting the arrival of the hangman.

When Birch did eventually make a sworn statement, he said that he was at Mrs Rae's camp on the day of the rape, and that he met two blackfellows further on, coming from the direction of Wivenhoe. Both men were "perfectly cool" and had no apparent heat from running. One of them, Billy Horton, he knew "perfectly well". Birch said Mrs Rae in the first instance said only that two blacks had assaulted her.

Chapter 3, A mailman's suspicions

ON FEBRUARY 12, 1862, Dr Henry Challinor, Member of the Legislative Assembly, Justice of the Peace and Coroner for Ipswich, wrote to Judge Lutwyche about the trials of Billy Horton and Kipper Billy.

The doctor said he had carefully examined Thomas Birch, the Burnett mailman, about the attack on Mrs Rae, and Birch had said he called at the Raes' home on the day of the assault. Birch said Mrs Rae had shown him some injuries and had said the assault had been committed by *two* blackfellows; that she recognised one whom she described and who was the Aboriginal man known as Stinkabed Johnny; and that the other was so disguised that she should not know him if she were to see him again.

According to Dr Challinor, the mailman said that after leaving the Raes he called at Pritchard's, where Pritchard told him that Stinkabed Johnny had been there and threatened him.

Pritchard had said there was another blackfellow he did not know with

Stinkabed Johnny, and that he, Pritchard, was prepared to shoot them if they came again. Birch told Dr Challinor he left Pritchard's in company with a butcher named Graves for Major North's residence, and within a few miles of there they met Billy Horton, whom the mailman knew well, and Jacky, North's black bullock driver.

The mailman said the distance between the Raes' hut and where he met Billy Horton was 11 miles.

Dr Challinor also wrote that Birch said Mrs Rae's husband was very drunk when he called at the Raes' hut; that a James McFadden was also at the hut; that McFadden told him that Mrs Rae only complained to him that two blackfellows assaulted her, that one of them was Stinkabed Johnny, and that the other was so disguised that she should not know him again. Dr Challinor told Judge Lutwyche:

With regard to Kipper Billy, I would observe that I was myself present when he was brought before Colonel Gray (the Ipswich magistrate at the time). Pritchard then made a statement to the effect

*that there was another blackfellow
with Stinkabed Johnny when the
Aboriginal threatened his life;
Pritchard said he did not remember
seeing this man before that day, but
believed it was Kipper Billy.*

Dr Challinor wrote that Mr Daveney, the Clerk of Petty Sessions at Ipswich, possessed "no maudlin sympathy" for the Aboriginal people, yet having heard Mrs Rae's first statement respecting the persons who supposedly committed the assault upon her, and the manner in which she exculpated Billy Horton when first brought before Colonel Gray, did not believe that either Billy Horton or Kipper Billy were at all implicated in the matter "from first to last".

"It seems to me a great pity that Mr Daveney was not examined for the defence," the doctor said. "It seems also that some steps ought to be taken to ascertain whether Kipper Billy was at Mr Bigge's station any part of the day the assault was committed upon Mrs Rae, Kipper Billy having made that statement to Colonel Gray before he was committed (for trial)."

Judge Lutwyche sent the doctor's

letter to the Clerk of the Executive Council, A.W. Manning, with a covering letter dated February 15, 1862, in which he commented:

I may at once state that if it had appeared in evidence at the trial either that Billy Horton was seen at a distance of 11 miles from Rae's hut within a short time after the commission of the alleged offence, or that Mrs Rae had been confronted with Billy Horton and said that he was not the man who assaulted her, I should have directed the acquittal of both prisoners. It is much indeed to be lamented that Mr Daveney was not called as a witness for the defence when he might have been subjected to cross-examination by the Crown Prosecutor; but if he can verify by affidavit what he seems to have declared to Dr Challinor to be a fact, the testimony of Mrs Rae as to the identity of Billy Horton is evidently not to be relied upon, and I shall humbly recommend that a free pardon be granted to both prisoners. If Billy Horton was improperly convicted, Kipper Billy, who was indicted for aiding and abetting him, must have been improperly convicted also.

The trial judge observed that the statement made to the mailman Birch conflicted with Mrs Rae's evidence as to the identity of Kipper Billy. "Mrs Rae said at the trial that Kipper Billy was naked, and had nothing over his face, while she is reported to have said to McFadden that the second blackfellow was so disguised that she should not know him again," Judge Lutwyche noted.

On March 19, 1862, the judge wrote again to the Executive Council:

I have attentively perused the supplementary evidence which has been taken, and I am of the opinion that the alibi set up by Birch has entirely failed. One important point, however, remains. Mr Daveney has not been examined, and I think the ends of justice require his testimony. He will be able to say whether it is true or not that when Mrs Rae was first confronted with Billy Horton, she said that he was not the man who assaulted her.

Judge Lutwyche did not say why Birch's alibi evidence failed. But by then the matter was academic so far as Kipper Billy was concerned – he had died violently 14 days before, allegedly felled by a prison turnkey's bullet.

Birch's disclosure that the white man, James McFadden, was present at the Rae hut when Mrs Rae was attacked, and the insobriety of the woman's husband, add interesting dimensions to her account of the rape. Birch said McFadden had told him Mrs Rae said she had been attacked by only two Aboriginal men and did not say she had been raped. He told Birch he had helped Mrs Rae into the hut. Although Mrs Rae was screaming loudly enough for her son to hear her on the other side of the river, neither McFadden nor her husband seems to have gone to her assistance, although she was being assaulted only about 30 metres away at the edge of the sawpit.

What if McFadden had taken advantage of Rae's drunken condition to attack Mrs Rae himself? She would have had to explain to her son and husband the injuries she had sustained and the condition of her clothing, and she was obviously, from her subsequent evidence in court, afraid of her husband's reaction to any suggestion that she had been raped. When asked in court why she had not complained of rape originally, she replied that she was aware of her husband's violent personality and did not want trouble.

The concoction of a story that Aboriginal men had attacked her would have been a convenient way of accounting for her condition without provoking any criminal reaction against McFadden. Nobody seems to have asked McFadden why he did not go to her rescue, although he must have heard her screams. Even when she went to Ipswich to report the attack to Colonel Gray, McFadden was kept right out of the picture. His presence at the Rae hut remained a secret until Birch exposed it weeks later after the two Aboriginal men had been condemned to death.

Another odd aspect of the story is the lack of any explanation for Mrs Rae's strange behaviour with the mare. Why was she trying to drag the horse *towards* the river, the direction in which the supposed attackers had escaped? And why did her son, who was approaching from the other direction, not see the Aboriginal men swimming across the river? Why would she not, instead of struggling inexplicably with the mare, have gone to the hut only 30 or so metres away where her husband and McFadden were then supposed to be? Mrs Rae must have known of McFadden's presence, as she was at the hut only minutes before preparing lunch. Was she trying to mount the mare to escape from the scene?

Chapter 4, Two men await their fate

THE "common gaol" where Billy Horton and Kipper Billy were lodged to await the pleasure of the hangman was Brisbane's second purpose-built prison.

Its dual stone cell blocks, surrounded by tall inner and outer wooden walls, held 96 prisoners in single cells that were only 2½ metres long and 2 metres wide. The prison stood from 1860 until 1883, overlooking Brisbane city from what was then known as The Green Hills.

In 1883 it was replaced by a new facility at Annerley that was to become infamous as Boggo Road Gaol. Boggo's predecessor on Petrie Terrace then became the Queensland Police Depot where generations of rookie policemen were housed and trained, and in the early 21st century has morphed again into the upmarket Barracks Precinct containing multiple theatres and fashionable restaurants. The Petrie Terrace gaol replaced the first Brisbane prison, which stood on the site of today's General Post Office and was the scene of a string of eight gruesome public hangings during the 1850s; four were Aboriginal persons.

When the first black judicial victim, Davy, was executed outside the old prison in August 1854, *The Moreton Bay Courier* seemed to think it was about time. Davy was hanged for the murder of a man named Trevethan at Wide Bay while Trevethan was handing out gifts to Indigenous inhabitants. He was accused of being one of several tribesmen who fell upon Trevethan treacherously and clubbed him to death.

The Moreton Bay Courier observed that about 50 white men had been murdered in the district and was impatient with people who had tried to persuade the authorities against hanging him.

"About 50 white men have been killed in these districts, without one such public example being made," the newspaper said after the hanging. "We consider that the executive acted with proper firmness and judgement in carrying out the sentence of the law on this occasion. The Aboriginal natives (*sic*) had so frequently escaped the punishment of their crimes that they had begun to look upon the sentence of death as a mere bugbear and a farce."

The newspaper also noted that "to the shame and disgrace of the town, a very large number of women and children were amongst the spectators".

One of the terminal events carried out in Queen Street was the bizarre public execution of an Aboriginal man named Dundalli, a warrior leader of his people's resistance against white settlement. Dundalli's end in 1855 was so revolting that the British Government ordered the cessation of public executions, making the Aboriginal terrorist the last person to be hanged publicly in Queensland. He had reputedly led bloody tribal raids on white settlers around Brisbane for 14 years before being arrested in 1854 then tried and convicted of the murder of a white settler and his pregnant female servant at a station on the Pine River nine years before.

A scaffold was set up in Queen Street outside the old gaol for the appointed hanging of Dundalli on January 5, 1855. Police constables and Native Police troopers surrounded the gallows to prevent any escape or rescue attempt as the condemned Aboriginal leader was led out to it.

A large number of his tribal supporters lined the scrub that still existed below Wickham Terrace and a crowd of whites waited for the big event in Queen Street. As Dundalli was led to the gallows, he called upon the tribesmen assembled in the scrub to avenge his death, and they responded with a loud cry as his body dropped minutes later through the scaffold trapdoor. It was at that moment that the hanging became a sickening bungle.

Dundalli was a tall man by Aboriginal standards. He stood more than 183 centimetres and was described later by the judge who tried him, Sir Roger Therry, as "the largest man I ever looked upon". Alexander Green, the seasoned official New South Wales executioner – he hanged 490 people in his 27-year career – who was sent from Sydney to hang Dundalli, made no allowance for his victim's unusual height, and used too much rope.

The hapless Aboriginal man's feet fell upon his pre-positioned coffin, so that Green, a runted 55-year-old former convict with a hideously scarred face, was forced to descend from the scaffold and drag on the man's long legs in a macabre dance of death until he strangled.

The Dundalli hanging was one of the last performed by Green, who was already mad at the time. Four months later he was committed to Tarban Creek Asylum – later Gladesville Mental Hospital – in Sydney. He disappeared through its gates and was never heard of again.

Despite the ban on public executions after the horrible death of Dundalli, the scaffold for the execution in 1859 of the aforementioned Aboriginal men, Dick and Chamery, was erected inside the prison yards in a position that deliberately made it visible from outside. *The Moreton Bay Courier* said in its report of the execution on August 6, 1859:

The gallows was erected in the gaol yard, and as it had been intimated from Sydney (Queensland was not to be separated from New South Wales for another four months) that it would be desirable to allow a few Aboriginals to witness the tragedy, it was deemed advisable not to screen the machine of death.

The Moreton Bay Courier said two Aboriginal men who were in the prison were brought to see the end of Chamery and Dick. "The elder's name was John Bull," the newspaper said, "and the younger, of whose cognomen we are ignorant, but who awaits trial for an attempt to commit a like offence for which the blacks suffered, trembled excessively and appeared frightened. After the bodies had been suspended for some time, they were taken down by Elliott, the hangman, and John Bull, the blackfellow, helped to put them into the coffins. They were shortly after taken away on a dray to be buried in the bush outside the burying grounds."

The horrible events that awaited the two Billys as they occupied cells on Brisbane's death row at the Green Hills were, therefore, hardly unprecedented. The Aboriginal people of southern Queensland had had 38 years to observe so-called white civilisation since the first convict settlers and their soldier guards arrived from Sydney at what is now Redcliffe in the sailing ship *Amity* in 1824.

They had quickly become aware of the births there soon after the first settlers arrived of two white babies – Amity Moreton Thompson, the daughter of a British soldier, and Charles Morton Miller, son of the first Commandant of Moreton Bay – and knew from those births that the whites were not Aboriginal people returned from the spirit world, as they had at first believed, but flesh-and-blood humans like themselves.

By 1862 free settlers had been arriving at the Moreton Bay settlement for 20 years, since transportation of recidivist convicts ceased in 1842. Many more whites had settled on pastoral land outside a 50-mile (80-kilometre) radius of Brisbane during the convict era by travelling overland from the south with their flocks and herds.

The Indigenous people in 1862 had long ceased to believe that firearms were some sort of magic, and many of them, while working for bush settlers or serving with the Native Police, had become highly skilled in the use of carbines and pistols. Mrs Rae's description of the rapist who attacked her as being dressed in a clean blue shirt and trousers indicates the extent to which the Aboriginal people had already adopted white ways, and Billy Horton's unaided address to the trial judge showed a considerable degree of sophistication. The two men awaiting judicial termination of their lives undoubtedly apprehended fully the awful end that awaited them at some still unspecified time, and no doubt bore the psychological weight of the knowledge as fearfully as any white man.

The mental terror that Kipper Billy and Billy Horton were subjected to seems to have been entirely unnecessary. As early as the day after they were sentenced, authorities were told that the two men might have an unassailable alibi for the time of the crime, in the form of mailman Thomas Birch who had not given evidence at the trial.

The Queensland Times reported on February 7 that Birch was willing to swear that on the day of the Fernie Lawn rape he had seen Billy Horton, whom he knew well, 11 miles away from the scene.

But Kipper Billy and Billy Horton were unaware that deliverance might be at hand as they awaited their fate in the grim stone cells of Brisbane Gaol. As condemned men, they spent virtually all their time locked in their tiny spaces.

For an hour or so every afternoon, after the rest of the prison had been locked down for the night at 5 o'clock, they were allowed to leave the cells in leg irons and chains to exercise in the deserted prison yard, but otherwise they had no contact with outside life.

The two Aboriginal men had been incarcerated thus for 28 days when Kipper Billy made a break for freedom. For 22 of those days the Government had been aware, via Dr Challinor's letter to Judge Lutwyche, that there might be serious flaws in the evidence upon which the two condemned men were convicted.

When a turnkey went to his cell to release him into the yard on the afternoon of March 5, Kipper Billy, who was sitting on a blanket that covered his legs, said he was sick. Leaving the cell door open, the prison officer turned back into the yard. As he did so, Kipper Billy rushed from the door and ran across the open space to a 4-metre wooden wall separating it from another exercise yard.

During the day, using the blanket for cover, Kipper Billy had ground the iron ring that linked his leg irons together on the stone floor of his cell until the chains separated. With strips torn from his blanket, he had then tied the chains to his thighs so that he would be able to run freely, and feigned illness during the unlocking of his cell.

As the prisoner headed for the inner wall, turnkey Richard Whitehead fired two shots at him but both missed. Kipper Billy continued to climb the fence until he was able to hang from the top by his hands and work his way hand-over-hand to the outside wall. Turnkey Edward Armstrong then came onto the scene. He said in sworn evidence before an inquest that when Kipper Billy ignored his orders to come down from the wall, he shot him through the head and his dead body dropped outside the gaol.

Chapter 5, The theft of Kipper Billy's head

GAOLER Samuel Sneyd was attending a funeral at the mortuary chapel of St John's Church of England in the nearby North Brisbane Burial Ground at Milton (now the site of Christ Church and Suncorp Stadium, formerly Lang Park) when he was told of the fatal escape attempt.

He hurried to the scene and saw Kipper Billy's body back inside the prison's B yard. It was there that he identified the prisoner, and it was there that Visiting Justice F.O. Darvall saw it before holding an inquest. No postmortem was held and there was no evidence describing Kipper Billy's wounds. Within hours the Aboriginal man's body was buried in unhallowed bushland that had been earmarked but not yet allocated as a burial ground for St John's.

The Visiting Justice reported to the Colonial Secretary the next day:

I yesterday evening held a Magisterial Inquiry in HM Gaol, Brisbane, touching on the death of an Aboriginal prisoner lying under sentence of death known as "Kipper Billy". From the depositions taken I am of the opinion that Kipper Billy died from the effects of a gunshot wound inflicted on him by Turnkey Armstrong, who in the efficient discharge of his duty shot him in the head as the only apparent means of preventing him from effecting his escape from gaol. The security of the Gaol as a place of imprisonment depends entirely upon the alertness and efficiency of the turnkeys, and it is satisfactory to observe that these essentials were not wanting on the present occasion.

Subsequent events show that the inquiry was a farce. The Visiting Justice apparently did not examine the body, or if he did, falsified his report as to the shooting of Kipper Billy. A simple reconstruction of the events from a distance of 150 years discloses that Kipper Billy could not have died from the cause the report suggests. The missing link in the tale came in the form of three graverobbers.

On the night of the escape, three men working by the dim light of an oil lantern opened Kipper Billy's grave and stole the Aboriginal man's head. The event was not unusual in itself. At that time the so-called science of phrenology, by which self-styled scientists claimed to be able to identify criminal characteristics in the shape and formation of the heads of offenders, was in vogue. The robbing of graves of men who had been executed was looked upon widely as a scientific necessity. But the taking of Kipper Billy's head was to prove exceptionally controversial.

The bodysnatching was said to have been led by a well-known Brisbane character known as "Old Tom", at the instigation of T.S. Warry, a chemist who ran a dispensary in Brisbane and who was both a Member of Parliament and a Justice of the Peace, highly respected positions in the 19th century community. As a JP, Warry sat regularly on the Brisbane Magistrates Bench.

It was not long before rumours of the midnight desecration of Kipper Billy's grave began to circulate. One story was that Old Tom had invited several dignitaries to lunch with him at his home, and that during this function he produced a partly boiled-down human head from a three-legged iron pot and declared it to be that of Kipper Billy.

The story said several of the guests lost their lunch but were able to see that there were no bullet holes in the skull. The cranium did, however, exhibit an indentation, and the story gave rise to speculation that Kipper Billy had not been shot, but had been bludgeoned with the butt of a turnkey's carbine.

Brisbane prison guards in those days were armed with .577 calibre Enfield carbines, which had a weighty military-style wooden stock. The butt of the Enfield was shod with a heavy brass plate, and speculation was that a blow from this had caused the fleeing prisoner's death.

There were other theories that the ball from Turnkey Armstrong's carbine had entered under the eye of Kipper Billy or through one of his nostrils and remained in the head, explaining the absence of both entry and exit holes.

It can be said with certainty that such

explanations are absurd. The Enfield Carbine fired a .45-inch 530 grain (34 gram) lead missile at a muzzle velocity of 900 feet (270 metres) a second, creating enormous kinetic energy that would have caused devastating damage to both flesh and bone when striking a human head at point-blank range.

This author[3] has in fact seen the damage caused to a human skull by a .45 calibre round. The subject had shot himself through the roof of the mouth with a 45/577 calibre revolver, and the damage where the missile exited through the top of his head was enormous. No such damage was evident on the head exhibited to Old Tom's luncheon guests, and no ball was recovered from inside the skull.

---

[3] Ken Blanch

Chapter 6, Church men seek some action

A FELLOW magistrate named Lewis Adolphus Bernays was the whistleblower who disclosed T.S. Warry as the instigator of the Kipper Billy grave robbery. Bernays informed two wardens of St John's Church, Henry Buckley and Shepherd Smith, that Warry had shown him a skull at Warry's house at the beginning of April and told him voluntarily the head was that of Kipper Billy.

The two church wardens considered it their duty to investigate but several more weeks passed before they did so. On April 21, *The Courier* published correspondence between the church wardens and the Colonial Secretary's office. Messrs Buckley and Smith first wrote to the Colonial Secretary on March 29:

> *In discharge of our functions as the Wardens of St John's Church, and the representatives of the members of the Church of England within this portion of the city, it has become our painful duty to*

report to the Government that an act, alike of wanton outrage to ourselves and revolting to the good feeling of the whole community, has been lately perpetrated by the violation of the sanctity of our burial ground, and the mutilation and part removal of the dead within its precincts. We seek the assistance of the Executive towards the discovery and punishment of all who have been concerned in a deed so abhorrent.

In consequence of rumours which had reached our ears to the effect that a skull had been exhibited in town said to be that of the Aboriginal man "Kipper Billy", lately shot in an attempt to escape from the Brisbane Gaol, and afterwards interred in the plot of ground granted to the Church of England for burial purposes (though not yet fenced in) we deemed it incumbent upon us to institute such investigation that would test their truthfulness, and accordingly we proceeded this afternoon in the presence of witnesses to disinter the body. Suffice it that we found the rumours too fully substantiated; and from the chain of evidence we have been able to assemble we (though grieved to be compelled to associate the name of a Member of Parliament and a magistrate with such a deed) cannot avoid the conclusion that a grave amount of suspicion attaches to Mr Thomas Symes Warry, of this city, of having been directly or indirectly implicated, inasmuch as, in addition to the requisite evidence to prove that the body after interment was disturbed and mutilated we have testimony borne by a magistrate of the territory (Mr Lewis A. Bernays) that Mr Warry, in his own house, more than a fortnight since, exhibited to him a skull, which then he (Warry) voluntarily declared to be that of "Kipper Billy".

That the whole Colony is deeply interested in the suppression of such repulsive misdeeds we are fully satisfied; the treatment of the remains of this Aboriginal man may be the treatment of ourselves, our relatives, our friends; and the offence in question, we submit, should be made the subject of public condemnation so marked as to prevent the probability of its recurrence. We are aware that in cases of this description complete evidence against the offenders is difficult to obtain, and that prosecutions frequently fail on technical grounds when no moral doubt of the guilt of the accused exists. It is possible that this may prove a case in point; but even so, we trust that the statements herein set forth, at all events so far as they affect the character of a Justice of the Peace appointed by the present government, will be deemed sufficiently serious to call for some investigation by the Executive – we hope it may be equally due to himself and the public, and we sincerely trust that he may be able to disperse the suspicion at present resting on him; failing which, however, we rest confident the government will take such steps as will meet the requirements of the occasion, and prove satisfactory to the public and the body on whose behalf we write.

The Colonial Secretary replied on April 16:

Gentlemen: I have the honour to acknowledge receipt of your letter of the 29th ultimo, bringing under notice the fact that the grave of the Aboriginal "Kipper Billy", recently shot whilst attempting to escape from gaol, had been opened, the coffin wrenched open, and the head of the deceased severed from the body and removed. The government have heard of this disgraceful outrage upon every feeling of propriety with extreme surprise and indignation, the more so as circumstances tend to place under grave suspicion Mr T.S. Warry, a member of the Legislature and a Justice of the Peace. In the opinion of the government, such an act is a misdemeanour of such character as to demand exemplary punishment, and they would urge upon you the necessity for making the most strenuous exertions to bring the offence home to the guilty parties. With you, as wardens, the duty of prosecution by criminal information *rests; and I am to convey to you the opinion of the Executive that no delay should be permitted to occur in bringing the matter before the proper tribunal.*

The Courier, which only a few weeks before had trumpeted its concern over a black man's life depending on the uncorroborated evidence of a rape victim, seemed to have a lot less concern for the posthumous theft of the same man's head, particularly if it were at the hands of a prominent citizen. In a tart editorial on May 3, the newspaper observed:

The criminal (Kipper Billy) was buried in a piece of ground which, of course, is unconsecrated but which, it would appear from subsequent events, had been promised by the Government to the Church of England for burial purposes. Owing to rumours current in the town some few days back, Messrs Smith and Buckley, Churchwardens of St John's, deemed it their duty to exhume the dead criminal's corpse, the head of which they found had been severed from the body and carried away. The result of their subsequent inquiries was that they wrote to the Government and accused T.S. Warry, MLA, chemist of this town, of being the despoiler. Their reasons for accusing Mr Warry were stated to be that Mr Warry had in his own house told a brother JP, Mr Bernays, that he had taken the head in question, and that Mr Bernays had forthwith come and voluntarily informed them of the above confession.

The Churchwardens further recommended indirectly that Mr Warry should be prosecuted in a court of law and deprived of his commission as a magistrate.

The Government, in reply, recommended the Churchwardens to prosecute, and expressed their regret to find Mr Warry accused of such a charge. Mr Warry has since written a letter (published in The Courier *on April 24) in which he does not positively deny the truth of the charge, nor does he confess it. He states his perfect readiness to meet the charge in a court of law but refused to acknowledge any accountability to the Church-wardens for his actions. He also reprimands those gentlemen for impertinence in their gratuitous recommendation that he should be dismissed from the magistracy; and finally, he condemns in severe terms the conduct of Mr Bernays as a breach of hospitality. Since this letter, the parishioners of St John's have passed a resolution instructing the Churchwardens to proceed in a court of law against Mr Warry, and here at present the matter rests.*

The Courier, which had so righteously defended the rights of Kipper Billy and Billy Horton when evidence of a miscarriage of justice began to surface, and declared that black men as well as whites should be entitled to those rights, had under-gone a sudden change of heart when it came to the robbing of a black man's grave. The newspaper declared that it did not regard the "obtainment" of Kipper Billy's head as any offence at all, the matter was a trifling one, and an everyday occurrence. It explained:

A chemist and apothecary, who happens also to be one of our leading citizens, a Member of Parliament, and a Justice of the Peace, was professionally desirous of ascertaining the effects of the gunshot, and accordingly procured the head. In this act there was no attempt at concealment, because it was never imagined that anybody would be so foolish as to make a fuss about it.

It is ridiculous to set up such a disturbance on such a flimsy pretext. The whole colony is one vast burial ground for blackfellows, and if it be a grave offence to obtain the skull of one, let us bring up all the culprits and have a special assize for the purpose of trying them, to be held (as it would have to be) when Parliament is not sitting.

The Courier thought it was reprehensible that the Colonial Secretary's office had asked Mr Warry to show cause why his name should be erased from the list of justices.

While Mr Warry might have been coy

about admitting his guilt publicly through the columns of *The Courier,* he was more humbly honest in a letter he sent to the Colonial Secretary about the matter on May 2. He wrote:

I was ignorant of any law existing to protect the bodies of persons dying in the manner of this criminal and buried in unconsecrated ground and without the rites of the Church. I may remark that during my residence in Queensland I have frequently had skulls of blacks given to me which have been used by me for scientific purposes in my profession, and I believe there was no harm in receiving them. I have to express my regret if I have impinged the Law in any way and trust this explanation will be satisfactory.

Warry's letter is remarkable in several ways. Weeks after Billy Horton, and therefore according to trial Judge Lutwyche also the now-deceased Kipper Billy, had been cleared of their rape convictions, Warry still referred to Kipper Billy as "this criminal". And although he regretted any transgression, the grave robber made no offer to relinquish the head or return it to the grave. The skull remained in his possession and was exhibited to many people in the ensuing years. Perhaps the most remarkable aspect of the grave robbing was the fact that Warry claimed to have retrieved the skull for scientific purposes. If that were so, he must have realised from the absence of bullet holes that Kipper Billy did not die from being shot in the head. Warry must have known that the prisoner was killed in some other way that had been covered up deliberately, yet as a Member of Parliament, magistrate and prominent Brisbane citizen he took no steps to disclose that the warders had conspired to perjure their evidence at the inquest and that the Coroner had given an outrageously incorrect verdict when he said Kipper Billy had been shot while trying to escape. Could it be that the black man's head was removed to *prevent* discovery of the real cause of death at some future official exhumation? The chemist was by no means so contrite about his part in the bodysnatching allegations of church wardens Buckley and Smith. In his letter published by *The Courier* on April 24 he said:

This correspondence, when divested of all its mawkish sentimentality and absurd exaggeration, amounts to this: that Messrs Henry Buckley and Shepherd Smith, the humble servants of the Bishop of Brisbane, transformed themselves for the nonce into detectives; that they went out to a piece of ground devoted hereto to the interment of felons, but which they allege to have been granted to the Church of England for burial purposes; that they there disinterred the body of the unfortunate "Kipper Billy"; that they found the corpse headless; and that – to use language that ought to be familiar to them – "from information they received" (the informer being Mr L.A. Bernays, a person whom I once remember to have been foolish enough to admit into my parlour on an equal footing with myself), they imagine a Member of Parliament and a Justice of the Peace, meaning your humble servant, to be the perpetrator of the so-called "enormity". Once and for all, I most distinctly refuse to acknowledge my accountability, either to the Bishop or the wardens of St John's, for whatever I may have done. I am prepared, when called upon, to defend myself in a legitimate way, but object most strenuously to be "called to the bar" by persons who are, without figure of speech, public servants. So long as I fulfil my duties as a magistrate and Member of Parliament to the satisfaction of the public in the one case, and my constituents in the other, I consider that I fulfil all that is required of me, and I object to having my public capacities violently dragged into the assistance of my calumniators. I can understand the animus by which one of them, at least, is actuated; and I can understand, also, the influence which is at work behind the scenes. For each of these I care not. As an independent citizen, I claim to be judged in this matter, and I wait with patience further action on the part of the wardens.

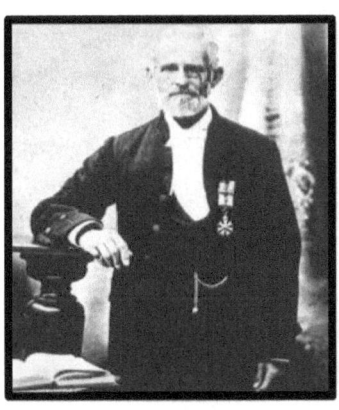

Lewis Adolphus Bernays was the first Clerk of the Queensland Parliament and the man who blew the whistle on the Kipper Billy grave robbery (State Library of Qld; #121468).

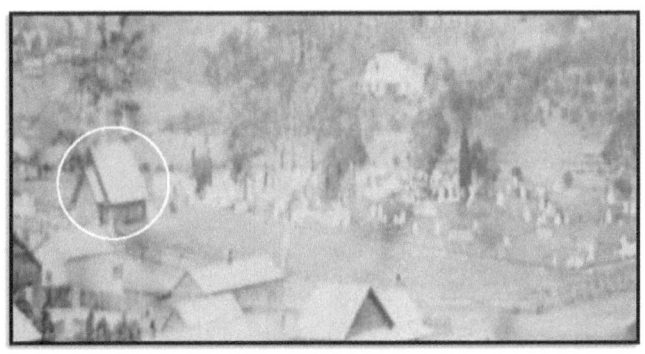

The mortuary chapel (circled) and burial ground of St John's Church of England at the North Brisbane Burial Ground, Milton, where Kipper Billy's grave was robbed. It is now the site of Christ Church and the internationally known Suncorp Stadium, formerly Lang Park. (State Library of Qld; #65399).

Chapter 7, A pardon for Kipper Billy's mate

WHILE THE hubbub over the death of Kipper Billy and the theft of the unfortunate man's head was going on, Billy Horton remained in his cell in the Brisbane Gaol still awaiting the attentions of the hangman.

But Billy was not alone on death row – a Chinese named only as "Tommy" was also awaiting the ministrations of the executioner. Tommy had been sentenced to death for the murder of a man named George Lang at Apis Creek, on the gold diggings near Many Peaks in central Queensland.

The gaol chaplain, Rev J.R. Moffatt, had tried to console Tommy to his coming fate, but the Chinese confirmed a disinclination to die right up to the hour of his hanging – the morning of April 2, 1862.

Workmen had spent several days erecting the scaffold for Tommy's execution. It stood in the middle of the prison's B yard, the enclosure from which Kipper Billy was trying to escape when he was killed. The macabre hanging machine was erected in full view of both the condemned men confined in B wing – and the hanging turned out to be a grisly affair. *The Courier* reported next day:

When the prisoner came from his cell, where he had previously been pinioned, he walked firmly to the foot of the scaffold by the side of the chaplain, but his features were very pale and ghastly in their aspect, and fear had evidently taken possession of the unhappy man. Arrived at the foot of the steps, Tommy knelt down with the chaplain while the latter read the prayers usual on such occasions, and remained quiet until the close, when he drew up one knee, laid his head upon it, and began weeping bitterly.

After the prayers were concluded, he moaned and cried piteously, and laid himself down full length on the ground saying "I won't die! I won't die!".

It was found necessary to carry him up the steps and get him on to the scaffold by main force, and the scene, as may be imagined, was sickening and horrifying to the last degree. The prisoner, who was apparently in a state of extreme mental agony, refused to stand upright, and the executioner had to adjust the rope round his neck while he was lying down on the drop, the prisoner still saying "I won't die! I won't die!". At length the fatal signal was given, and all the unfortunate man's protestations were ended by his being launched suddenly into eternity. Death was instantaneous, and the body was shortly afterwards cut down and removed for burial.

The Courier added, as if by afterthought: "We have omitted to mention that, as on former occasions, there were a number of persons in the trees outside the gaol enclosure, watching the proceedings."

The persons in the trees were not the only spectators. Billy Horton, although locked up in his condemned cell, had a full view of his fellow prisoner's end through the grille above his cell door. He was to say later that he thought the hanging machine the workmen were erecting in the yard outside his cell was for him. The whole affair of watching another man die by the judicial rope while awaiting his own turn must have been an awful ordeal for Billy, who knew that he was innocent, but thought he was going to hang, nevertheless.

His amazement when prison officials opened his own cell only an hour after Tommy's ordeal and told him he was a free man can only be imagined. *The Courier* reported the day after Tommy's execution:

> *Hardly had the revolting spectacle of yesterday morning been presented to those who witnessed it, when a scene took place which was almost as gratifying as the other was horrible. Billy Horton, one of the two Aboriginals who were sentenced to death for committing a capital offence on the person of Mrs Rae near Ipswich, was set at liberty, His Excellency the Governor having been pleased, in his case, to exercise the prerogative of mercy and grant him an absolute pardon.*
>
> *The welcome missive arrived soon*

after the execution took place, and Mr Blakeney (the then Assistant Sheriff) at once proceeded to the cell of Billy, who had been taking a bird's eye view of the previous proceedings (the hanging of Tommy) through the grating over the doorway of his cell. He had apparently been prepared for the intelligence to some extent by hopeful anticipation, but his countenance was overspread with an expression of joyfulness which very rarely is witnessed in everyday life. Mr Blakeney and the chaplain both informed him that the Governor had pardoned him, and that he was free to go, whereupon Billy – who evidently had an opinion of his own as to the justice of the proceedings, and who speaks very good English – affirmed that he was never guilty of the crime, and that his accuser had not told the truth.

In a few minutes after Billy had been told of his good fortune the heavy irons on his legs were stricken off, and as the last rivet fell the poor fellow heaved a long sigh of relief, showing that however calm he might appear externally, there were emotions going on within. Billy says he shall stay in Brisbane and does not seem to approve of the idea of going back to the scene of his capture, and of the crime of which he was wrongfully convicted.

We learn from Mr Alderman Petrie that he knew Billy Horton when quite a lad, and he was then one of the most well-disposed and well behaved of the Aboriginals frequenting the streets of the town. No long time had elapsed after his release before Billy might be seen roaming through the streets in a cast-off volunteer uniform, recounting his triumph to those who recognised him, and appearing as happy as any man might be expected to be under the circumstances. The pardon in this case is, as before stated, absolute, and has been granted, we believe, on the ground that circumstances have come to light since the prisoner was sentenced, to show that clear proof of his identity was not established at the trial. There cannot, we should think, be two opinions as to the prerogative of mercy having been wisely and justly exercised in this case.

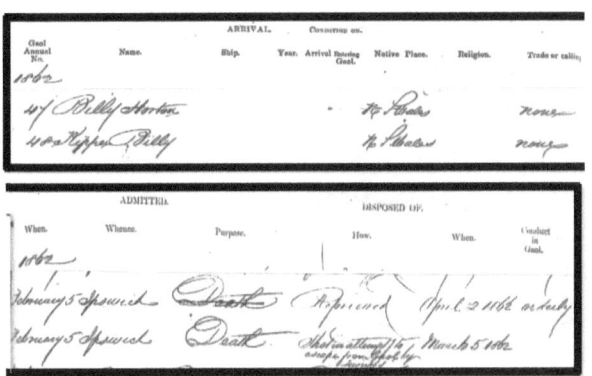

The entry in the Brisbane Gaol Register recording the admission of Billy Horton and Kipper Billy admission on February 5, 1862, and their death sentence. The register shows that Billy Horton was reprieved on April 2, 1862, and that Kipper Billy was "shot in attempt to escape from gaol by turnkey" on March 5. (Qld Government, Department of Justice and Attorney-General.)

The minutes of Executive Council meetings held between February and April reveal that Judge Lutwyche first addressed the council about the possibility of Billy Horton's innocence on February 18 and a stay of execution was granted.

Kipper Billy, although still living, was not mentioned. The matter was again raised on March 18 and deferred until Judge Lutwyche was able to give his advice on the matter, as he had not yet examined the new evidence regarding the alibi for Billy Horton.

On April 1, the judge recommended that the Executive Council issue a free pardon and release Billy Horton from the gaol on the grounds that his "identity with the actual criminal is so questionable". Neither Billy Horton nor Kipper Billy had been advised of the stay of execution. It is reasonable to assume that had Kipper Billy been so advised he would not have attempted the escape that led to his death and the theft of his head.

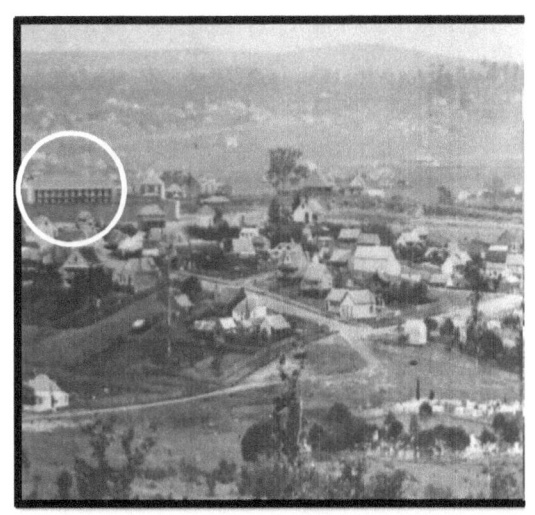

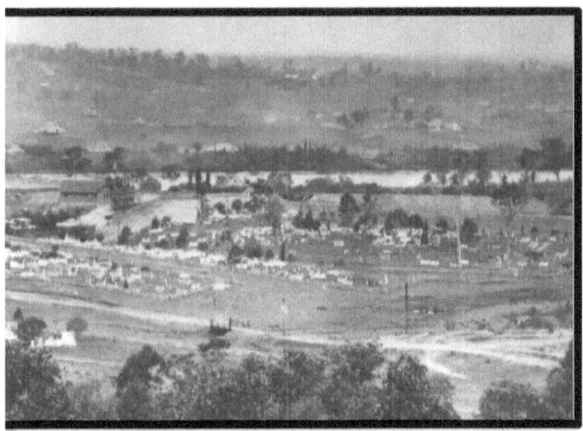

The scene of the awful killing of Kipper Billy. On the far left of the first picture is the old Brisbane Gaol (circled) where he died trying to escape an unjustified death sentence for aiding and abetting a rape that he was never involved in. The gaol overlooks

the old North Brisbane Cemetery, Milton (now Suncorp Stadium), from where Kipper Billy's head was taken by grave robbers. His fellow supposed offender was given a full pardon and escaped hanging after Kipper Billy died. (State Library of Qld; #162681).

Executive Council minute of April 1, 1862, in which Billy Horton was granted a free pardon. (Qld Government, Department of the Premier and Cabinet.)

Chapter 8, 150 years of shame

BUT WHAT of poor Kipper Billy? There was no mention of any posthumous pardon for him. Although he was clearly as innocent as Billy Horton, he remained branded as a criminal. Brisbane historian Nehemiah Bartley was to write in *The Brisbane Courier* 30 years later of "Kipper Billy ... another notorious black criminal". Billy was still regarded as guilty then, and modern crime history writers before now had not dispelled this injustice.

According to Bartley, whose account was published in *The Brisbane Courier* on May 31, 1892, under the heading "BLACKFELLOW CRIMINALS", the Upper Brisbane River was the scene of Kipper Billy's "exploits". The indefatigable chronicler of Brisbane's early contemporary history wrote: "He had an eye for white female beauty, and one handsome lady, the wife of a rich squatter there, carried a small revolver for his benefit after hearing how he had spoken of her."

If Billy had such a reputation with white women that they armed themselves against him, it seems extraordinary that Mrs Rae had never heard of him before she was attacked.

Bartley wrote of Kipper Billy: "He was a daring fellow, and after his capture he scaled the wall of Brisbane Gaol and would have got away, but a bullet from the carbine of Warder Armstrong killed him when on top of the wall, and strange to say no hole could be found in his head or any part of his body, and it was supposed that the bullet entered under his eyeball and remained in his skull." There was no suggestion in Bartley's account that Kipper Billy was ever pardoned.

Another old Brisbane identity, A.G. Bailey, replied to Bartley's account with a letter to *The Brisbane Courier* on August 9:

> *I was intimately associated with the two persons (now also departed) who secured the head (Kipper Billy's) for examination. Mr Bartley says it was thought that the bullet from the warder's musket entered by the nostrils and so caused death. Now, if that were the case the bullet would, at short range, have passed through the*

cranium. That it did not is pretty certain, because there was no perforation of the skull. I am sure of this, because I have seen the skull scores of times. Again, had the bullet remained embedded in the brain it would have been discovered. Now the object of "Old Tom" was to find out, if he possibly could, what it was that killed the native, for there was no external mark. The necessary steps were taken ... and the result showed an unmistakable indentation above the right ear, caused no doubt by the brass-bound heel of a clubbed musket. The inference, therefore, is that the warder fired at the black while he was on top of the gaol wall, the shot missed its mark, the darkey fell or jumped, and before he could recover from the shock and escape the warder had descended from his lookout turret and clubbed him with the butt of his musket. It could be seen plainly enough when the skull was cleaned, and a remark of "Old Tom's" that the gaoler "could not hit a haystack" was verified.

The suggestion that Turnkey Armstrong descended from a guard tower and clubbed Kipper Billy with the butt of his carbine is untenable.

Construction of the stone wall that replaced the wooden fence commenced a few weeks after Kipper Billy's attempted escape. *The Courier* reported on April 12, 1862, five-and-a-half weeks later, that the wall's foundations had been partly excavated and a temporary tramway built to convey the stone from punts on the Brisbane River to the gaol.

The photograph of the gaol reproduced in the previous chapter shows the prison as it was at that time. It had no towers on its 14-feet (4-metre) high wooden outer wall. Turnkey Richard Whitehead said in his evidence to the inquest: "Turnkey Armstrong, who was waiting at the foot of the fence, shot him the first time his head became visible at the depression of the fence."

Bailey's letter prompted a response from Bartley that provides a vital clue to what really happened to Kipper Billy. The old Brisbane historian wrote to *The Brisbane Courier* on August 20:

On the same day that he (Kipper Billy) tried to escape from Brisbane Gaol was the funeral of Mr Lachlan McLean, the father of Alderman McLean, and it was attended by a large number of citizens to the cemetery at Milton, for Toowong was still a wilderness then. On their return from the burial, several people were astonished, as they passed the new gaol at Green Hills, to hear the sound of carbines firing and to see a blackfellow on top of the wall. They realised matters at a glance, and some of them, who were constables and warders, made improvised weapons by tearing up some of the massive survey pegs which marked the newly laid out Crown lots on the Petrie Terrace that was to be, so as to be ready to apply them to the blackfellow's head so soon as he dropped from the wall, when he fell suddenly, and as they found, fell dead, and as the fall could not have killed him at once they searched for a wound. Mr Cox, who picked him up, is of the opinion that the bullet went up one nostril, and not (as doctors thought) into the eye orbit. One voluble old Italian, greatly scandalised at what he considered the too promiscuous and dangerous firing that took place, was loud in his denunciation of "thim assassins" as he termed the warders in the execution of their duty.

This account suggests that what really happened was that when Turnkey Armstrong fired at him and missed, Kipper Billy dropped to the outside of the wall. As he lay winded, or perhaps unconscious from the fall, one of the "constables and warders" among the passers-by hit him with a heavy wooden survey peg. Kipper Billy would have been an easy target for the law enforcement officers assembled there.

Reconstruction suggests that the prisoner fell with his back to them. The "unmistakable indentation" in his skull above the right ear suggests that someone wielding a heavy object hit him with a sideways blow from the right, a natural blow for a right-handed person. Bill Kitson, a widely experienced surveyor and bushman who became curator of the Queensland Museum of

Lands, Mapping and Surveying before retiring in 2008, said the heavy hardwood survey pegs used by surveyors in 1862 were 18 inches (35 centimetres) long and tapered from 4 inches (10 centimetres) square at the upper end to a fine point at the other. Such an object would have made an ideal club capable of killing a man instantly at one blow and leaving the "unmistakable indentation" on Kipper Billy's skull above the right ear noted by A.G. Bailey. Kipper Billy, it seems, was murdered in cold blood as he lay disabled from his fall and unable to pursue his escape or defend himself, and colleagues of the warder or policeman who did the job tailored and perjured their evidence to provide a massive cover-up for the crime.

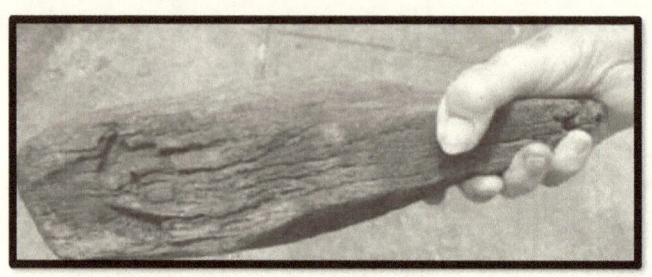

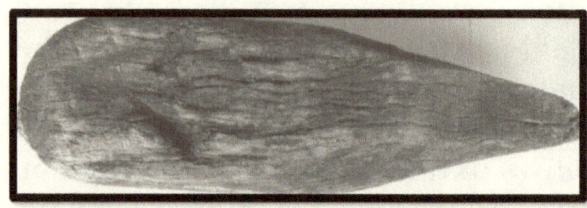

A pair of weathered survey pegs similar to those used at the time of Kipper Billy's escape. The survey peg becomes a deadly weapon with enough weight to kill at a single blow when grasped at the pointed end. Pictures by Jim Spurdle.

Chapter 9, What happened next

THE *Brisbane Courier* reported the death of Thomas Symes Warry Esq, "a citizen well known and much respected in this town", on Saturday, August 20, 1864, almost two-and-a-half years after the death of Kipper Billy. It said:

Mr Warry was taken ill on Sunday and since that day no hopes were entertained of his recovery. He expired yesterday morning at his residence on Spring Hill. Mr Warry, after being for a considerable time in trade in this town as a chemist, retired from business some two or three years ago. He held for a brief time a seat in the Legislative Assembly as member for East Moreton in the first Parliament, and was at the recent election for North Brisbane, which took place on Saturday last, an unsuccessful candidate. During his political career Mr Warry was generally a supporter of the present government.

Mr Warry was a well-educated

gentleman and a genial companion. Under a somewhat bluff and eccentric manner, he disguised a benevolence and philanthropy of disposition which practically was developed in numerous ways. He was an active supporter of all public charities, and in private any distress requiring relief was rarely brought under his notice in vain.

Many in this community will have reason to regret his loss and will miss his presence. We believe he will be buried this day in the ground appertaining to the Church of England, of which he was a member.

Thus, the mortal remains of Thomas Warry joined those of Kipper Billy, whom he had made headless, in the same burial ground and remained there intact until a mass exhumation in 1913 made way for the park that has become Brisbane's premier sporting ground.

The Warry remains were reinterred at Toowong where they are now unmarked. There is no record of Kipper Billy's body being exhumed, and the eventual resting place of his head remains a mystery. According to Aboriginal lore, the black man's spirit cannot rest peacefully without it. Perhaps, in the dead of night when the last hurrahs of some epic sporting event have subsided, Kipper Billy's restless presence haunts the green playing field of Lang Park, or Suncorp Stadium, or whatever name white men now give the former Milton burial ground, to this very time.

Mrs Jane Rae bore a son named Samson some time towards the end of 1862. The infant, whose birth was not registered, died at Little Ipswich (now West Ipswich) from inflammation of the chest on October 2, 1863. According to the death certificate he was aged eight months and Joseph Rae, a sawyer, was his father.

The *North Australian and Queensland General Advertiser* reported on August 22, 1863, that Joseph Rae had appeared before the Ipswich magistrate on the previous Thursday, about six weeks prior to his son's death, for "being found drunk in the public streets". He was sentenced to eight hours in the cells or a fine of 15 shillings ($77 today) and threatened with up to two years' imprisonment if he was caught again, this being his third offence within 12 months.

James McFadden, the white man who was present at the Rae camp at the time of the supposed rape, but who did not give evidence at the trials of Kipper Billy and Billy Horton, was identified by *The Courier* on November 26, 1862, as a sawyer who was fatally struck by lightning at Fassifern some weeks earlier.

Chapter 10 ... And then ...

THE PORTRAIT of Kipper Billy as a criminal we have just read continued when, as recently as 2012, Jarvis Finger included both Billy Horton and Kipper Billy in *A Cavalcade of Queensland's Crimes and Criminals: Scoundrels, Scalliwags and Psychopaths,* his anthology about Queensland crime and criminals of the colonial era. In recounting the story of their convictions and the pardon of Billy Horton, he neglects the point that Kipper Billy was also innocent.

The exception was Brisbane barrister Stephen Sheaffe, who noted that Kipper Billy had not been pardoned posthumously in his analysis of the "tragic injustice" suffered by the two Aboriginal men in the Royal Historical Society of Queensland's 2001 *Clem Lack Oration.* But more than 150 years later in 2015, Kipper Billy, *sans* head, still lay unpardoned in an unmarked grave somewhere beneath Suncorp Stadium.

No one knew where his stolen skull was. And the official register of the old

Petrie Terrace Gaol, preserved in the Queensland State Archives, still records in successive entries made in 1862:

No.	Name	When admitted	Purpose	How disposed	When	Conduct
47	Billy Horton	February 5		~~Death~~ Reprieved	April 2, 1862	Orderly
48	Kipper Billy	February 5		Death	Shot on March 5, 1862	Attempt to escape from gaol by turnkey

In May 2015, author Ken Blanch wrote:

It's time the Queensland Government reviewed the case and corrected the record ... and for the Suncorp Stadium authorities to remind its hundreds of thousands of sports fans of the place where an innocent man lost his head.

He was later advised by the Attorney-General of Queensland that he should petition the Governor of Queensland to exercise his Royal Prerogative of Mercy in this case.

Three years, and more than a century, later, Kipper Billy was pardoned by then-Queensland Governor Paul de Jersey, on September 20, 2018. No longer would Kipper Billy be named in official records as a "black criminal who died while trying to escape his lawful sentence". That Kipper Billy was owed a legal and unconditional pardon by the people of Queensland, and that his kin are owed a heartfelt "sorry", was always beyond doubt.

After all, he was accused of aiding and abetting the supposed crime of Billy Horton and, as the judge who sentenced him pointed out, if Billy Horton was innocent then Kipper Billy must equally have been so.

And it was no ordinary pardon: it was announced on the social media platform *Twitter* (now renamed as *X*) on September 20, 2018, after years of petitioning by this reporter with support from others who also wanted to see justice finally done.

Sources

Queensland State Archives

Item ID2917: Register of male and female prisoners admitted – HM Gaol, Brisbane Register, 3/1/1850-3/2/1864.

Item ID845334, 1862: Minutes Executive Council.

Item ID84756, 62/739: Letter from Sheriff's Office advising that Kipper Billy was shot while attempting to escape from Brisbane Gaol.

Item ID846757, 62/904: Correspondence relating to case of Regina v Billy Horton. Includes deposition from Mr Daveney, Judge Lutwyche's notes from the trial and evidence from the trial.

Item ID846759. 62/1358 : Correspondence relating to the robbing of grave in the burial ground of St John's Church, Brisbane.

Books

Beckett, R & Beckett, R 1980, *Hangman: the life and times of Alexander Green, public executioner to the colony of New South Wales.* Nelson, West Melbourne, Vic.

Finger, J 2012, *A Cavalcade of Queensland's Crimes and Criminals: Scoundrels, Scalliwags and Psychopaths.* Boolarong Press, Moorooka Qld.

Journals

Sheaffe, S 2006, 'A Tragic Injustice — The Trial of Kipper Billy and Billy Horton', Clem Lack Oration delivered 16 August 2001, in *Journal of the Royal Historical Society of Queensland,* vol. 19, no. 5, Feb., pp 824-840. Informit.

Newspapers

The Brisbane Courier, 31 May 1892; 9 August, 1864; 20 August, 1892.

The Courier, 6 February 1862; 17 February, 1862; 3 April, 1862; 12 April, 1862; 21 April 1862; 24 April, 1862; 3 May, 1862; 26 November, 1862.

The Moreton Bay Courier, 6 August, 1859.

The North Australian and Queensland General Advertiser, 22 August, 1863.

The Queensland Times, 7 February, 1862.

Personal communication

Bill Kitson, Curator Queensland Museum of Lands, Mapping and Surveying 1982-2008.

Vital Records

Death Certificate for Samson Rae, 2 August 1863, Queensland Registry of Births Deaths & Marriages, Brisbane.

Websites

Civil War Wiki.net, '1853 Pattern Enfield Rifle-Musket (P53)', civilwarwiki.net/wiki/

State Library of Queensland, www.slq.qld.gov.au

Thom Blake Historian, 'Historical monetary value calculator', www.thomblake.com.au

Wikimedia Commons, 'Baker's Map of Moreton Bay 1846', commons.wikimedia.org/wiki/ File:Moreton_Bay_1846_after_Baker_w ith_additions.jpg

Acknowledgements

The author acknowledges with utmost gratitude all the help given to him by colleagues, former colleagues and voluntary researchers in the preparation and production of this book.

In particular, he thanks his late partner, Jean Baxby, for her encouragement, and Ken's daughters, Kelyn Flynn and Marie Blanch, for their editorial and research assistance, and granddaughter, Julia Flynn, for her technical advice. Thanks to Thom Blake for his assistance and to Jim Spurdle who provided the survey pegs. My appreciation goes to Aunty Raelene Baker and Betony Bickford who took the time to read the manuscript and give me valuable feedback. My deepest thanks go to the staffs of the State Library of Queensland and Queensland State Archives, especially the Aboriginal and Torres Strait Islander Community and Personal Histories Branch, for their support and advice.

More True Crime by Ken Blanch

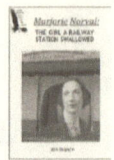

Marjorie Norval: The Girl a Railway Station Swallowed

Ken Blanch investigates the disappearance of prominent social identity, 29-year-old Marjorie Norval, from Brisbane's Central Railway Station on November 11, 1938.
Order online soon from Strictly Literary, http://www.strictlyliterary.com/

The Rampage of Killer Kast: Terror on the Terrace

In December 1955, Karl Kast shocked and devastated Brisbane's medical world when he killed two prominent orthopaedic surgeons and injured one in their Wickham Terrace rooms. Ken Blanch covered the story for *The Brisbane Telegraph* and re-examines the crime in this casebook.

Order online from Jack Sim Publications: www.jacksim.com.au

The Taxi Driver Killer: The Southport Murder

In May 1952, a blood-stained taxi was found at Southport. The driver, Athol McGowan, was missing. Nine days later, his body was found more than 100 kilometres north of the murder scene in Moreton Bay. This was the first murder that Ken Blanch covered for the *Telegraph* newspaper in Brisbane and in this re-examination of the investigation and trial, he raises serious questions about the conviction of Arthur "Slim" Halliday, a small-time habitual thief who was sentenced to life imprisonment for the murder.

Order online from Jack Sim Publications: www.jacksim.com.au

Who Killed Betty Shanks? Is the Wilston Monster Still Alive? (Revised edition)

In September 1952, 22-year-old Betty Shanks was brutally murdered as she walked from the tram stop near her home at Wilston after attending night classes in the city. Her killer has never been caught. Ken Blanch covered the case for the *Telegraph* newspaper in

Brisbane and after 60 years he re-examines the investigation and subsequent confessions. He raises new possibilities based on information that was available to police at the time but ignored.

Order online from Jack Sim Publications: www.jacksim.com.au